Working Woman Poetry

poems by

Claire L. Frankel

Finishing Line Press
Georgetown, Kentucky

Working Woman Poetry

*Dedicated to my great-grandparents,
Cecelia Strauss Obstgarten and her husband,
Chenninah Obstgarten who left the Austro-Hungarian Empire
in the 19th century to come to America*

Copyright © 2020 by Claire L. Frankel
ISBN 978-1-64662-245-0 First Edition
All rights reserved under International and Pan-American Copyright Conventions.
No part of this book may be reproduced in any manner whatsoever without written
permission from the publisher, except in the case of brief quotations embodied in
critical articles and reviews.

ACKNOWLEDGMENTS

"Deskbound" has been previously published by *Oberon Magazine*

Publisher: Leah Maines
Editor: Christen Kincaid
Cover Art: Claire L. Frankel
Author Photo: Bachrach Studios
Cover Design: Elizabeth Maines McCleavy

Order online: www.finishinglinepress.com
also available on amazon.com

Author inquiries and mail orders:
Finishing Line Press
P. O. Box 1626
Georgetown, Kentucky 40324
U. S. A.

Table of Contents

East River Drive/ FDR 1
A Doodle and then…Amethyst Sky in New York City 2
New York Public Library 3
Fantasy #131 4
My Apple Farm in Winter 5
December 2016 6
Where the Heat Can Make You Crazy in 5 Minutes 8
Deskbound 9
What I'll Miss When I'm Dead 10
Safe At Home 11
What Do Women Want? 12
Writing When Tired 13
Tagkonic Autumn 14
The Baptist Reconsiders 15
1950 16
She Said to the Classroom of Girls 17
Cold Weather 18
August 2014 19
Retirement Gift 20
Perfume 21
Days Inn Monmouth County (Bryan's Funeral) 22
Americans, All of Us 24
The Cemetery 25
1991 26
Cheney, Resurrected 27
Be Gone 28
One by One 29
2013 30
I Used to Walk to Work 31
Life 32
Accounts Receivable 33
Is Any Mayor Listening? 34

East River Drive/ FDR

What is a working woman's life?
To walk out exhausted at 9 pm
for a first breath of cold air.
To look at the bridges in the snowlight.
A crumpled face looking at
the diamond-strung bridges
From a taxi up the FDR.
Drive slow, my man.
The finest diamonds in New York
swing low across the bridges—
draped o'er East River bridges.
Carry me to my casket
on the other side of work!

A Doodle and then…Amethyst Sky in New York City

Diamond bracelets
On amethyst sky
Diamond bridges
On amethyst sky
Make rooms on the bridges
And the people walking back and forth
Arm in arm exclaiming,
"Look at the lights!"
"How beautiful
Oh."

Two days in a year
We have perfect weather
One in the Spring
One in the Fall
A jeweled night for walking the bridge
And sighing to the river
Under a diamond bridge
Under an amethyst sky
My love.

New York Public Library

This is my beloved place
the worn old oak
the writer's face
who came before me.

This is my civilization
the stacked volumes
and their cross keepers.

How could I ever leave?
I will haunt the stacks
forever with a grin,
a chocolate bar
and a Sondheim lyric sheaf

La, la   la, la,   la la   la la

What do I need for inspiration?
Only the old desk
a blank paper
a leaky pen
all is golden
in the winter.
Writing and singing,
Writing and singing
Pushing away the grave.

Fantasy #131

I know how to be Poor
Late rent
Living with Other People
Beans and dogs for dinner (or no dinner tonight)
$5 for the gas tank
Making $357 a month L_A_S_T.

I know how to be Middle Class
Working 24 by 7
Or pretending to ….or aspiring to
A love life ruled by Anxiety
(If I invest time in this man
Will it damage my career?)
The mortgage and the groceries paid for
And the business suits and the makeup
Annual trips to doctors rarely reimbursed
By corporate "coverage."
Real life squeezed into short weekends.
Jimmy took to drink and I to poetry.

I could learn to be rich.
I've had glimpses
A week in St. Barth's
with lunch on the beach.
3 hours of hair, makeup, cocktail dress and heels
For a turn at the Opera
A donor's midtown coop of 5 bedrooms and 5 baths.
The driver holds the packages
My tall great-aunt clicking down the hall
With her short housekeeper running after her
Insisting "Madam, Madam!"
[Why didn't she leave me her pile?]
She was rich.
Was she happy?
Did it matter?
When you subtract the Anxiety
Life is so much easier
Life becomes manageable
I could learn to be rich
But don't bet on my chances.

My Apple Farm in Winter

I'm glad for snow; it brings
No point to nagging that the side trees need a prune
No way to move the prunnings down the row
Only listen for the north wind's tune
Now inside chores and short days slow
It's the memory of petals' glorious perfume
The anticipation of a drunken bloom
That makes us tolerate
The snow after snow after snow after snow
And then it goes
And then it's June.

December 2016

Nothing inspires me
Sitting in the sterile shiny high-rise
I can watch the weather
I can do my assigned tasks
I can watch my words
I can keep my head down
There are different rules for women and men
Women must give bad news in a sweet way
and be perceived as "collaborative"
Palatable for Management
who know neither the business nor the technology.
Men can demand and curse
Belittle and sneer
Give heart attacks to lower ranking men
And never be blamed.
They don't go to the funerals
Afraid the widows will attack.

In the higher echelons, everything is rosy
And the money rolls in.
All news is good news
No one dares to offer different.
Flailing projects curtail their deliverables
and declare success.

Management is glad
"Thank yous" echo in the email
January bonuses are zero.
After all…The top 300 men need
Their millions. Who will pay?
Not you. Not the Shareholders.
Only the employees.
Working, working,
Working, working,
You can hear the lash
Even if you don't feel it on your skin
(You will be outsourced next quarter.

You will be downsized next quarter.
Work, work.
Work, harder.)

In the higher echelons, everything is rosy
And the money rolls in.
All news is good news
No one dares to offer different.
Flailing projects curtail their deliverables
And declare success.

Where the Heat Can Make You Crazy in 5 Minutes

Americans are masters of Euphemisms
"Paradise Valley" Yeah, of 110 degree deaths.
Dehydration Lane is more like it;
Heat that surrounds and invades
And is inescapable. Sweating, sweating, sweating.
The a/c wheezes and blows intermittently
Makes an old Russian want to drive
Straight into the tourist river.
In the meantime, the old man takes his last breathe.
Oh, we have asthma and we have moved here for our health
People say.
Oh, we have asthma and we've moved here for our health,
People say.
They take their dying breathes between the a/c whirrs.

If one thousand Phonecians turn on the sprinklers
To water their lawns green 360 days
Where does the water table go?
Is Phoenix green so that the old Comanches die of thirst?

The weddings go on between the young folks.
They've dotted the i's and crossed the t's.
Education—good job—earned money—lived together for x years
The wedding goes on
The parents are joyful or relieved or depressed
And then life takes over.
He's married his third girlfriend because
It was the right time in the universe, and
She lobbied like crazy for marriage.
His childhood sweetheart—she's married and divorced
With 2 kids.
30 years later, lobbyist dead and sweetheart divorced,
They are back together in front of a Rabbi
With a new Ketubbah.
With 20 years remaining they decided
The first was the best……after all.
Heat makes people crazy and swells the feet.
Once your feet are swollen, the brain no longer functions.

Deskbound

When you are deskbound
Poetry is the only possibility
You can start a novel
Or a non-fiction
On your Corporate Edition of WORD
But weeks of DELIVERABLES
(Now! Now! Finish it!!)
Will wear you down
And remove your focus.

A poem is a burst
A starlight
A break through
So clear, so happy
So breathtaking.

Unbound.

What I'll Miss When I'm Dead

Summer plums
Purple, sweet and dripping
Ice cream cones
The sugar ones
Here in the Village or in Italy
Filled with leaves of
Pistachio, Swiss Chocolate Mocha, Blackberry.
Ogunquit beach
The Mystic Outdoor Art Show
Sailboats lining up to pass under the bridge
The Metropolitan Museum of Art
How high the ceilings !
The stunning
The breathtaking
The heart breaking
Alexander McQueen
His soul laid bare
First, I missed him
Then, he missed me.
Monet's dream of lily and water
And more lily, more water
We are in the blue green water
The Louvre
The Dance in the City and
The Dance in the Country
To realize why people were shocked
When there is nothing really to be shocked about
The couple look at you, breathing
Same height
You can see them sweat
They are you
Dancing in a Paris café
Dancing in a crowded garden
On a hot summer night.

I will miss
A poem
You know which one.
The one in my heart.

Safe At Home

Up in the country
I sleep with the bathroom light on
In case of a break-in
I'll see the terrorist's face
After ADT starts shrieking
And 30 minutes before the police arrive
(They have a long drive).

Here in New Jack City
There's no need for a night light
I pull up my shade
The whole of Murray Hill is there
Sparkling and gleaming
You can see us from Outer Space
And it would take an army
To get past MY doormen!

What do Women Want?

This is what I want
That I not have a useless life
That I not have a useless death
That I looked upon the Earth and it was good
That I was able to do one kindness
That I assuaged one sorrow
In all my useless work
That someone, somewhere benefitted.

Writing When Tired

I'm writing when I'm tired
You know the feeling—
you've put in 10, 11, 12 hours
at your slave ship
and now you've come home…
determined to write a Truth.
Some truth.
Some evidence of thought
and life beyond your manager's orders
Some evidence of civilization.

Tagkonic Autumn

It is so glorious
To be alive
And to be able to see
The Tagkonic autumn

It really doesn't matter
Which road north
You take from the City,
The Thruway or old Tagkonic or 22.
An hour north
To Paradise.
The steep rolling hills
The soft rolling hills
In their Autumn furs
Of orange-yellow, green and red
As the highway narrows north
The golden boughs drape over it
Like the bedcurtains of
An upscale honeymoon.

At some point I'll be dead
And never see this luxury again.
But not now.
Now is glorious
And the leaves are printed
With your name.

The Baptist Reconsiders
After & For Dorothy Parker

Forty years in an office
Designing data
For indifferent traders.
I may as well drink.

All my money spent on art
And life in Manhattan.
(Consider Manhattans.)
I may as well drink.

One week by the sea, then
Back to the canyons.
The Borough is boiling.
I may as well drink.

Oh flowers, oh seaside, Oh gunquit
Gone in a blink.
I may as well drink.

1950

One tiny girl
On a giant beach
Under an endless sky.

Does she have a future?
Will her parents crush her before school does?
Will her school crush her before society does?
Will hatred of women carve her life
Or will she be oblivious and free?

Each life has such potential
Most parents make it their business to crush it
Be practical ! (Aim lower) Be practical (Aim lower)
You're not good enough!

RPI Instead of MIT
Albany instead of Yale
Nurse instead of Doctor
Secretary instead of Executive
You will get married and have children
As if boys don't.
And then they wonder
Where all the angry women came from
In this land of the free and home of the slave.

She said to the classroom of girls

They had memorized over 100 silly songs
And so she said to the classroom of girls
Name 10 African-American women of achievement
Not singers, not dancers, not actresses, with all due respect
Since those doors, if not wide open, were ajar.
And they could not.
So here are 10—memorize these:
Sojourner Truth
Harriet Tubman
Lorraine Hansberry
Ida B. Wells
Rosa Parks
Rep. Shirley Chisholm
Maya Angelou
Oprah Winfrey
Dr. Shirley Jackson
Dr. Mae C. Jemison
Now look up what they contributed
To our civilization! Memorize that!

Cold Weather

My family loves the cold weather
True Mongol, true Siberian
All of our infighting happened in heat
Humidity makes us angry and terminal.

Violence is forbidden
Since we left the Tzar's Army.
Silence is the violence
       And Distance.
One living in Arizona
One in California
One in glamorous New York.

Still, the cool weather makes us civilized
Once again
"Come for lunch! We'll go see the armor at the Met!
And they all wonder, 'Why we like the armor so much?'
And I explain, "Once upon a time
we wore it."

August 2014

Two white-sailed sail boats
Far out beyond the white foam
Past the waves foaming at the shoreline.
Eight children wading in the low tide.
The setting sun illuminates the hotels.
A duck quacking .
How much better
Can it get than this?
I wish the clan were here
But everyone has their own schedule
And I command no one.

Retirement Gift

The old Filofax sits on the desk
Fat, analog, worn, stuffed with
Notes, pages, lists, griefs, small victories
Ready for its retirement cleansing
Debriding, debasement.
Do I need any of these firms' numbers?
Phone.
I stopped sending faxes in 1998.
I stopped using the Arpanet even earlier
It became the Internet….in case you didn't know
Will I be sending Bank of America a Christmas card?
Never.
Why do I need their address?
Can I remove this page? Should I just remove this listing?
Then there are the friends who have died.
If I toss their addresses and phone numbers, will I still remember?
Remember.
As long as someone remembers, you still live.
Should I buy a new Filofax and start over?
I need new friends, more friends.
Or should I put it all on the Internet…personal file….people I want to see again
To laugh, to argue politics, to discuss cooking and restaurants, to sit with
I think about the billions of people who have died and the 'Filofaxes'
All their friends
Who I will never meet
To live now, you must remember now
Remember as much as you can, and live life.

Perfume

I raise apples—not cows
For 2 weeks in May
My farm has its own perfume.

It is a heavy scent and
Carried by the breeze
The gates of heaven

Some spring in my life
I won't have to work
In a sealed-off stuffy office
I will sit here and gulp the breeze
And know I am in heaven.
It's all I need
of heaven.

Days Inn Monmouth County (Bryan's Funeral)

When young men die
What happens to their souls?

The constant energy tackling projects
Embracing all who knew them
You didn't have to know them
They radiated energy
>>Impatience
>>Purpose
>>Direction
The willingness to fix the world
Shoulder to the wheel
Lifting all children they ever met

NOT the "White Man's Burden"
But Men's joy in life
>>In work
>>In family
Oh the souls, souls
Now splayed across the universe

What happens to little children
When their father is gone?
It depends
If he left any money …….or not
If he left a large family …..or not

Money buys food and shelter
>>Better schools
>>Holiday presents
>>College
And then you are on your way
Along with the hole in your heart.

Large family brings caring or abuse
It's impossible to predict
Good Uncle, bad Uncle
Kind Aunt, Indifferent Aunt
Injured Mother

And the young widow
Raising children—
alone or with family and friends
2 a.m. panic attacks
Months pass, years pass
To grow a career or not ?
To marry again or not ?
To live here—to move away ?
I don't have answers
This is a lot harder than derivatives.

Americans, All of Us

To the farm, my tiny niece
Where we will eat chicken and peas
Under my fragrant apple trees
And talk of Dominica and Ceylon.

To the farm away in secret upstate
Where the secret police will never go
Though the snows are much smaller than Aral
And the neighbors - our vigilant militia.

To the farm, my tiny niece
Where you can ruckus in fragrant apple trees
And learn to be secure and brave
My future President.

The Cemetery

Hinehni, your lone strange grandchild on the edge of 60
Visiting the relatives in their carefully manicured rows
For the New Year (The rest of the year, they're left wild.)
Oh raise a glass Uncle Phil
I brought your favorite Chivas
I never drank it while you were alive
Let's raise a glass together
I'm here to report –
Your great nephew was bar mitzvahed last Saturday
His sister 3 years ago
I am the only one in the family who respected them both
As you would have
Well, they are teenagers now
The half and half parents
Anxiously/ curiously rising to the occasion.

People astonish me
I saw your daughter
Anorexic or addicted who knows ?
She thinks she's a supermodel and says nothing.

I saw my brother
You wanted to reconcile parents and children
But now it is left to my generation
To speak to each other.

It's a good thing you never saw 9/11 or
Much of Bush 2.
You would have picked up your revolver
Silent since the War.
Like the old Mongols we are—
On our horses—armed to the teeth—
Ride and fight, ride and fight
A lifetime for Chingas.
25 years for the Tzar.
Now we fight with words and silence
 and injure each other.

1991

They're getting Cheney ready
For his second coming
Left Ventricle!
Right ventricle!
Volley and thunder
Out of the valley of death
Where the rest of us go
He comes charging on a black steed
Harbinger of more war and more war.
Only his relations escape
The rest of us must defend democracy
Whether it is threatened or not
He sees enemies.
Slaughter is the only response to his vision.
Well, the country needs clearing
Of poor men.
No jobs for them anyway
And the unemployed pay no taxes.
Cheaper to bury them at Arlington
And express profound regret
Turn the cameras away

They're getting Cheney ready
For his second coming
A vague republican rolls towards the White House
In need of counsel
He of two minds
Any man but a half white man and
This one's persistent.

The second coming approaches
And we must prepare
Send all the young people to Canada
And buy stock in war machines.
We'll outsource the next war
For the sake of democracy.
We'll order mojetos on our terrace in Florida
And watch the end of the show.

Cheney, Resurrected

What do I care for dead soldiers?
They pay no taxes
Wasted taxes
Wasted on child care centers and women's rights
The only good dollar is used to build a smarter bomb
A smarter bomb is worth a million dollars
You there! Give!!
Are you not a patriot?
Stupid citizens and their stupid pleasures
Like golf and bowling and
quilting and synagogue dinners.
These funds belong to your government—to me!!
You stupid citizens squealing left and right
About health insurance !
Did I have to worry about paying for my new heart?
(My new pretty purring heart.
Left ventricle! Right ventricle!)
Of course not—YOU paid for it!
As well you owe me!
I was your "government servant!"
You paid to restart my heart
When for war crimes
You should have paid
To stop it.
I adore my stupid Americans
Paying and paying
Praying and paying
"They are well trained, your masses,"
Said Mao Tse-tung
Yes, my heart swelling with pride
We give them a basic education
Not enough to gather facts and reason
Just enough to salute the slogans
Yassir knew that.
"We should take lessons from you," he said.
"You have," said I
Curling my lip upward when I am pleased.
"And should you need a new heart, Mr. Chairman,
I offer Baylor and the top of the list."

Be Gone

I am waiting for them to go
Filling rooms with nonchalant comment
Casual asides
Conversation they believe to be reasoned
I am polite
And I wait for them to go.

I am waiting for them to die off
The ones who didn't want a girl
Who wouldn't waste their money
on the girl's education.
One left on my Mother's side
One left on my Father's side

Old hatred dies soft
When few recognize it
I am waiting for them to die off
I am waiting for them to go.

One by One

One by one we appear
The brilliant, the talented, the not so
Childhood takes SO LONG to be over
Year after year after year of school
And then
There we are—an adult!
We must decide
A marriage or not
A career or not
A place and a time and a menu
Every 15 minutes, it's breakfast!
Older and older and older
For the lucky
Ah, we are so lucky
Then one by one we disappear.

2013

I was 63...and then... 68
I expect to live as long as Aunt Sue
Who was 104 and then 106
Or at least to her brother's 95.
Jewish Mongolians don't die—
Even the ones who are Russian Orthodox
(inside joke)

Why are all these blue veins appearing
Just below my surface
I'm too young.

My friend's children run screaming
Around the side table and
All through the house.

I comb my hair
And see their daughter at 19
Their son at 17
The grandparents safely tucked
Into their boxes.
Life not long...or fair.
But these are my friends
And I'll outlive them all—I know it
I must strap on my side-arms and prepare
To meet the Angel of Long Life.

I Used to Walk to Work

The high performance cross-town bus will take me
4 stops and down 4 flights
To the downtown subway N, W train—never high performance
Up one flight and down one flight
To the under Hudson Path to the ramp and the escalator
Then walk to the high-performance office building.
I get into my high-performance elevator to the 18th floor.
I check into today's reservation for a high-performance workstation
I find an empty workstation.
I am exhausted.
I am low performance for the first hour of work.
Then I have a muffin and a cup of coffee
And it's back to the grind.
Is it any wonder that my most clever
Database designs happened when the commute
Was 15 minutes?

Life
  My Life in my Teens and in my 60's

Long
Long Long
Long l o n g
Long l o n g
Long

Ummmm.

Short
Short Short
Short _{short}
Short _{short}
Short_____Short
Short Short Short
Too.

Accounts Receivable

I close the kitchen cabinet
But it snaps back at me
Someone was here while
I was in D. C.

Someone picked through my library
While I was testifying
Who would know which door to use
And the alarm code?
Was one of my farm hands a plant?

Did you find what you were looking for
My spy of spies
Not too many commie books?
Nothing on totalitarianism
Make America Green again?

Would 4 Yiddish cookbooks disqualify me?
How about histories in 4 languages?
Don't forget Hebrew; that makes 5.
My struggle with Hebrew
Too many ch'a-ch'a-ch'as.

In your haste to find -- pot? –evidence? –what?
You broke a small side lamp
And now my act of sly revenge
I mail its replacement bill in broad daylight
To Ms. I. Cypher
J Edgar Hoover FBI Building
Washington, D.C.
To be paid within 30 days or legal action will ensue.

Is Any Mayor Listening?

We had a really lovely day
Little Sofii and I
It was summer
We were wearing white shorts
                And white sneakers
We strolled Central Park and
Had chocolate ice cream cones
For three dollars each and
A cup of coffee for two dollars each.

Then we walked all the way down
To the Lexington passageway
Food extravaganza, for more.

I picked up a box of rugelach at Eli's
But it was $14.95 so the nice fellow
                Put it back.
We saw cups brimming with watermelon
                Across from Elis.
                They were $11.99 per lb,
                and watermelon is heavy
Lovely small chicken pot pies beckoned at Dishes
But $9.99 each is too much for us
Then cheeses at $9.20 per slice!
And beautiful crab cakes at the seafood stand
We could afford the free samples of gluten-free shrimp salad, so yummy
So on the bright side it was
A taste of shrimp salad, a chocolate ice cream and a coffee.
I would like to give Sofii an entire meal
But as long as we live in New Jack City
It's scraps.
Is any Mayor listening?

Ms. Frankel was artistic and literary as a child but became fascinated with math and science in the 8th grade. She attended Rensselaer Polytechnic Institute and graduated State University of New York at Albany with a degree in Physics. Since graduating, she has worked, full time and over time, in the fields of Data Modeling, Data Architecture and Data Engineering. Her initial work was in Early Response Systems for nuclear power plants, but since moving to New York City in 1981, she has focused on database design for financial services computer systems. She manages groups of engineers and vets every entity-relationship-diagram (database design.)

Ms. Frankel has always written short poems, in addition to her engineering work. She has written during coffee breaks, during boring corporate meetings, during lunch time and down time. Her 60 years of scribbled poems are still scattered all over her house and work notebooks, making it difficult to assemble them in one place. Nevertheless, she persists in gathering poems written over the years. She is delighted to share some of them with you now, thanks to the Finishing Line Press.